Versus.

Versus.

Pure Slush Vol. 5

Claudia Bierschenk
Ron Campbell
Carolyn Cordon
Howie Good
JP Reese

This second edition published April 2015, edited by Matt Potter
First edition published February 2013

Poems copyright © the individual poets

All rights reserved by the authors and publisher. Except for brief excerpts
used for review or scholarly purposes, no part of this book may be reproduced
in any manner whatsoever without express written consent of the publisher or the authors.

Pure Slush Books
4 Warburton Street
Magill SA 5072
Australia
Email: edpureslush@live.com.au
Website: http://pureslush.webs.com
Visit the Pure Slush Store: http://pureslush.webs.com/store.htm

Cover design by and copyright © Matt Potter

ISBN: 978−1−925101−84−3

Also available as an eBook:
Kindle ISBN: 978−1−925101−34−8 / ePub ISBN: 978−1−925101−85−0

A note on differences in punctuation and spelling

Pure Slush proudly features (both online and in print) writers from all over the English−speaking world. Some speak and write English as their first language, while for others, it's their second or third or even fourth language. Naturally, across all versions of English, there are differences in punctuation and spelling, and even in meaning. These differences are reflected in the stories *Pure Slush* publishes, and it accounts for any differences in punctuation, spelling and meaning found within these pages.

for

Susan Tepper

who would have

something to write

on all these topics

Foreword

Poetry often gets a bad rap. Usually from me. But I know some poets now – more than I used to – and one day I thought, what if *Pure Slush* published a poetry anthology … ?

No one would expect it …

It could be fun …

And if nothing else, I might learn something …

But how? I didn't want just any old poetry anthology, so the wheels started churning and double meanings are hard to resist and *verse / verses / versus* popped into my head and so too did differing or opposing opinions and so, very quickly, *Versus. Pure Slush Vol. 5* was born.

Devising the list of topics was not difficult – fun and serious but universal – and the poets have all been published before on *Pure Slush*, if not their poetry. But thought was also given to their diverse styles and what's more, when approached with the idea, they all said *yes!*

What makes great poetry, and what makes it different from great prose? For me – and this happened with a number of these poems when I first read them – I think, oh, I don't get it … and then I go away … then come back and read them again … and think … and then they reveal themselves.

And that, really, is the power of poetry.

Matt Potter, editor *Pure Slush*, February 2013

16 drink
24 seasons
32 convenience stores
38 marriage
46 chores
54 personal grooming
62 budgets
68 interior decoration
78 gender
86 public transport
94 church
102 raising children
112 politics
120 guilty pleasures
128 future

drink
seasons
convenience stores
marriage
chores
personal grooming
budgets
interior decoration
gender
public transport
church
raising children
politics
guilty pleasures
future

An American in Belgium

1
Clocks imprisoned in stone began ticking.
Everybody born here seemed to know what that meant.
I hadn't spent much time in skyscrapers,
holding the black receiver to my ear.

2
The rain fell.
I watched through the train window.
Cows were kneeling in a field
out of a mistaken notion of humility.

3
A hand
had washed ashore
outside Antwerp.

Somebody mentioned
the Congolese;
somebody else,
the Russian mafia.

"Can you taste
the honey?"
another new friend asked,
the table crowded
with bottles
& bulbous beer glasses.

I said I could.
I couldn't.

Howie Good

Club Mate *

Big-eyed girls with glossy lips
clack-clacking high heels
staccato on station platforms
they giggle at skinny boys
whose window pane glasses
are too large for their beardless faces.

They're crowding subways and doorways
freeze their bony knees outside
important clubs for hours
with eagerly indifferent faces
the air teeming with
dark American vowels and
high-pitched Englishness.

In the grey netting of small hours
empty shells of trendy drinks
is all that's left of them

until the bottle collectors appear
in second-hand East German coats
and give-away woolly hats
they know where to look

filling filthy bags
clank-clanking in the dawn.

Claudia Bierschenk

---

* Club Mate: soda drink containing caffeine, currently very "hip" in Germany.

Recipe

Love.
Take 1 part dragonfly juice.
1 part evaporated ice,
1 wisp of smoke
And add a heaping spoonful of lateral gravity.

Combine 1 part delighter fluid,
1 part joy venom
And some complicated syrup.

Add 3 awkward glances,
2 catcalls
And 1 hubba—hubba.

Add a twist of fate,
A float of hope,
And 1 drop of flopsweat.

Stir until dizzy.

Rim glass with fingernail clippings or the crushed lenses of a pair
    of Victorian opera glasses.
Garnish with a little umbrella of parchment upon which is
    written a suicide note or a sonnet.
Pour into a mug of burnished moonstone or a hypodermic.

Best served in an inny belly button.

Ron Campbell

Achieving Sobriety

After he wandered from the house,
baby Cory scattered himself like bread
on the winter waters of Lake Mendota.
We carried him home, diaper dripping, lips blue.
Mary, still sotted, pulled on ashen clothes.
She rocks at the window most days, watches for birds.

When Alex went out for a pack of Pall Mall,
his tires drew two runnels through the October grass.
He planted his Buick in the Dempsey's big screen.
Come spring, the St Augustine grows far too long,
as a legless Mack Dempsey can't mow.

Before Carmen went dancing, she glugged down
two bottles of Lancer's Rose. The alley flared cold
against her bare back as three men took turns
beneath a rain whittled sky.

We found secret bottles behind bookshelves
and chairs. Grampa lay in his vomit and decayed
for days. A young couple bought what was left of his home,
their life packed in boxes from Sparling's Fine Wines.

JP Reese

Our little secret

It wasn't the grog, I tripped over my dog
and now the hound's gone bush.
I'd not been drinking, but heavy thinking
and the fall's a secret, so shoosh!
No need to tell, they'll scream and yell –
they don't need to be told a thing.
Family and bosses, and government tossers –
say too much, they'll wail and cling.

So let's keep it quiet, no need for a riot,
it wasn't that bad and I'm perfectly fine.
I had a little sip, then the dog made me trip,
it's our little secret, yours and mine!
You're my friend, and the tale's at the end;
I know that you know, there's nothing to say
to hubby or son, so let's have some fun,
there's this pub I know, we can kick up and play!

Carolyn Cordon

drink
seasons
convenience stores
marriage
chores
personal grooming
budgets
interior decoration
gender
public transport
church
raising children
politics
guilty pleasures
future

Crash

I was listening to silence
Wondering if silence was listening to me
When we were both interrupted
By the crash
Of a snowflake.

Ron Campbell

Affliction

The city has covered itself.
Under the blanket
the congested
draw patterns over
fragile white skin.
Summer has no such pleasure.

Claudia Bierschenk
translated from the German by Desmond Shortt

Autumn

The field lies stubbled.
Its carapace brittles
under November's drowsy
song. My hands chill,
and I warm them
beneath my arms.
I stand on the edge
of this empty earth.
The jacket I chose
Doesn't ease the shivering,
but I stay because
I have come here
to understand. Out here,
this emptiness,
this barren soil
reflects all loss,
its truth painted wide
across the gleaned wheat.
This earth speaks to me
of my own inevitable
and solitary finish.
My lover's face
found autumn, too,
pale cheeks washed
in amber half–light,
soft whiskers bristling,
eyes closed in a final leaving.

Perhaps he was a boy again
chasing crows
from the corn green fields,
blue eyes lit by a summer
just coming on.

JP Reese

Autumn Sonata

Sometime during the night,
adolescent miscreants
decapitated the mailbox,
and the dog chewed up
the only thing worth reading.
God hid in the attic,
semi-white and waxed,
a color referred to
as Lighthouse Shadow.
The leaves have more or less
made up their minds to die.

Howie Good

Why did the snake cross the road?

Was it there as a warning
or just a sign of season's change?
Whatever the reason,
the creature pounded my heart,
bang bang bang,
as the shiny, undulating
metre and a half of it
disappeared
into the grass
on the left side,
the sinister side,
of the road.
I bid you farewell, snake,
may we never, ever
meet again…

Carolyn Cordon

drink
seasons
convenience stores
marriage
chores
personal grooming
budgets
interior decoration
gender
public transport
church
raising children
politics
guilty pleasures
future

the inconvenience store

Set out by experts, with every item
strategically placed to ensure maximum
inconvenience.
The things you really need,
the staples – bread and milk
are they right there, waiting for you
when you first arrive?
Bread and milk? No, they're not,
but you're invited to consider
the wonders of the store instead –
specials, new things you didn't know
you needed, are there first up,
in your face, strategically placed
to tempt you, tickle your fancy
with fancy food, and amazing products
that produce, what?
Not much really, if you think about it,
but thinking about it isn't encouraged.
Thinking about it is for losers,
the ones who'll miss out on the best new thing,
because it doesn't measure up,
when they measure up the benefits
of yet another processed,
chemical–laden and fatty item of non–food,
available in store, for their inconvenience.

Carolyn Cordon

Catch Trap

She's worked in the business since she was thirteen when daddy inserted his blood-crusted key. Years later, as paint peels, the woof and warp cants, he leaves her his ashes to spread on the clay. She won't leave the counter; it's all Marlee knows. When men stop to pay her, she's easy with smiles. She's served bankers, bus drivers, and one or two bums. Night watchmen occasionally toss her some cash after filling their tanks, but they all disappear. Handprint smudged doors turn the few passers-by into silent cartoons Marlee watches all day. She hawks Parliaments, hot dogs, and ice-clustered Cokes, but her loyalty, even on discount, won't sell. Posted signs ask the rough men to please wipe their feet, but frayed edges soon crumple, ink fades in the sun. Mud clotted work boots leave streaks down the aisles like striped bruises she hides under uniform sleeves. After midnight she padlocks the entryway doors, escapes to dark barrooms, then whiskey-fueled sleep. In her dreams there's a bed of red feathers and dew, bejeweled mosses drape grottos, frame purple lagoons. She climbs a steep cliff toward the blue chenille sky where trapezes sway chained to foam-headed clouds. It's a space where a father's fists can't beat a child, and hope never wings from a punch-swollen eye. She alters her grip on the links as she swings between bars sloughing silver and bits of fool's gold. Gaining speed, Marlee leaps from one man to the next, terrified of the space in between.

JP Reese

To the Blue

1

Spring breaks out in fires, hair streaked with blood, a black postcard shoved under my door. It's the same as seeing anorexic coeds floating through the sky above campus. Please do not feed the cats, the sign on the hurricane fence says. Dipshits and dimwits cluster according to internal laws. My heart makes a fist. I'm full of forces whose existence can't be proved.

2

The falcon was sometimes called a sparrowhawk. A woman's body might be searched, but it can't give that information. The moon rises before day has even ended. Always remember, light and shadow never stand still. I take the road that the arrow indicates I should. The leaves tremble with the effort to suppress an onslaught of tears.

3

I turn down the alley behind the empty strip mall. Angels in dark glasses sit along the edge of the loading dock, swinging their pale legs and waiting. The fruit they tried lies discarded on the ground. I taste rather than smell smoke. The most mysterious thing is a fact clearly stated. I'll be found – perhaps not until years later – wandering the streets wearing only one shoe.

Howie Good

Transit

In the airport I count;

1 Cocktail bar
1 Hot dog stand
5 Mobile phone shops
6 Duty free shops
11 Restaurants
12 Boutiques
no bookshop.

With 5 hours and 20 dollars to spend;

1 Coffee (black)
1 Chicken wrap
1 Bottle of water
1 Salad.

All of human life can be seen in the airport in transit;

buying, what is unnecessary
eating, out of boredom
waiting, for the exit.

Beyond the concrete there is the illusion of a city.

Claudia Bierschenk
translated from the German by Desmond Shortt

Inconvenience Store

I opened an inconvenience store

It's kind of hard to find.

It's at the end of a one way street

And it's not online.

I opened an inconvenience store.

I thought you should know.

The hours are sporadic

And listed below.

Ron Campbell

drink
seasons
convenience stores
marriage
chores
personal grooming
budgets
interior decoration
gender
public transport
church
raising children
politics
guilty pleasures
future

Operators

Get married today.

Here's what you'll receive:

The driest of kisses.

The longest of sidelong glances.

Shoulder blades sharpened to perfection

And coffee cooled by the silences between sips.

But that's not all.

You'll also get:

Someone to cry with.

Someone to cry because of.

An expert blame game scorekeeper.

And real time hands on 24 hour driving instruction.

But that's not all.

If you act now you'll also receive:

Apologies through gritted teeth.

Advice at the top of its lungs.

Winces disguised as smiles.

Smiles disguised as winces

And laughs given like little wrapped candies.

But that's not all.

You'll also get:

Stabs of indifference.

Throat strikes of tenderness.

Little exhales weighed by the ton

And custom ribcage hand rests.

But there's more:

Sweatpants and flannel crumpling bumpily where
    fishnets once lured.

Accusations written in the code of unwashed dishes.

Compliments equipped with luggage racks.

And sighs as soft as bludgeons.

Operators are standing by.

Ron Campbell

night time struggle
(a Shakespearean sonnet)

The poems I write in my head, approaching sleep,
the words that tell of my thoughts and feelings for you,
are words I desperately, justly, want to keep,
they're from my heart, honest and surely true.

But sleep is my seductive, precious need,
my body knows it, leads away from verse.
Brain and body argue – which to feed?
My mind resists, and struggles, with a curse.

My husband next to me is unaware
of the nightly tussle occurring in our bed –
and sleeps, content. It seems to me unfair –
he rests, but my fight goes on, body or head,

head or body? He would say I should
embrace night's sleep. If only, if only I could ...

Carolyn Cordon

Love Surrounds Us Like a Posse in Bulletproof Vests

I'm a ghost seated before a blank mirror.
You're equal parts light & dark.

I'm a prescription that nobody can decipher.
You're whatever pill may cause drowsiness.

I'm empty lots & the basements of abandoned buildings.
You're the honeycombed blue mountains of night.

There are so many more stars than I remember there being.

Howie Good

Ghosts

Your phone has been disconnected
yet somehow you manage to call them
from your denouement in Florida.
You need someone to cry to,

your unending troubles barb
into the fabric of their thin, boy—man
skin. They cling for days afterward
to the meaning behind your call,

search for their own reflections
in the shining fish hooks of your words.
They shovel through the shit and stink, hoping
to claim the man they imagine still hovers

beneath the mire. Your second wife
has tossed you out. Tired of 8 am toasts,
she flings you and your empty pockets to the dirt
outside and slams the door, pours herself

a celebratory flute of champagne,
leaves you with nothing but a hollow ringing
in your skull, a used car, and a passport sporting
a blurred photograph with its rictus of a smile.

I wonder if your bottom lip still aches
where I punched you twenty years ago
in the blackest of nights when you tore
at my nightgown with your Miller Lite

hands, the boys still babies, dreaming down
the dusky hallway, drunken monsters hovering
above their heads. Even then they knew
no one would ever save them.

JP Reese

Marriage

She waits in the Tesco car park,
while he cracks jokes with the kids.

In the car they don't talk,
so she's mouthing place names
that echo an ancient tongue:
Perranporth, Padstow, Zelah.

They drive past thatched cottages
surprised by the sea around
the next corner, the UK's top forty
is the soundtrack to their journey.

She can see herself come back here
next year, cycling, walking, horse−riding,
drinking cider from the can in front of the gas fire.

The bed in the cottage is small
but big enough so their toes don't touch.

Claudia Bierschenk

drink
seasons
convenience stores
marriage
chores
personal grooming
budgets
interior decoration
gender
public transport
church
raising children
politics
guilty pleasures
future

Rush hour

Where every morning I saw his
arse pass by on a bike,
today a father waves his child goodbye.
That child used to be him.

Fat cow: every morning
in the same chair,
she's been sat there
my whole life.

Claudia Bierschenk
translated from the German by Desmond Shortt

Not a Housewife

'Clean your keyboard, take time away
from the screen, and get it nice
like a housewife should.'
Yeah OK, I said I'd do it – typed up
the words, clicked on the links – they can't
come check, that's what I think. If they can
then I blew it, but ah, what the heck!

Daily Challenges come in from way out there,
words on the email, say what I'm supposed to do –
this one's stupid, my keyboard's clean
or clean enough, anyway, and that's what counts.
Clean enough's good enough
as far as I care, the letters don't stick
and that's all that matters.

I'm not a good housewife, I admit it,
and don't care – dog hair and dust, well, so,
what's your point? It's not too dirty,
it's fine, it'll do – we're all well in this house,
so it's healthy enough. This Daily Challenge
has only happened once, next time
it comes 'round, I'll wipe it away …

Carolyn Cordon

The Day I Don't Wake Up

The day I don't wake up
I won't have to brush my teeth.

The day the rigors of life give way to the rigor of mortis,
The day the bacteria, held at bay by my thumping motor
      all these years hear in that last thump the signal to ravage
I won't have to return any emails.

I won't have to pay that bill
Gas up that car
Check that calendar.

My calendar will be an ocean of ice.
Day after day of blank.
Day after day of me not being.
I'll have heard and made my last complaint
The day I don't wake up.

The day I don't wake up
I won't have to go to the DMV.

The day the calcium ions of my body, deprived of oxygen,
Leak into the muscle cells and turn them into little fists,
And my capillaries bloom blue in the bag of me
I won't have to fix a faucet or put on a tie.

Someone else will put on my tie
The day I don't wake up.

I will not turn to dust
The day I don't wake up.
For dust is dry and wet is death
Like life.

The day I don't wake up
Is the day my poetic license expires.

Ron Campbell

Topos

I have spent five years preparing to leave this city,
a flat, dry place of endless roofs that layers its citizens
in safety from the great unwashed, those others
with bat—shaped eyes who hover on the edges
just below them——those who have fallen from the ceilings.
I am falling, too, plummeting from the middle class.
I do not know where I will land. The roadway beyond
the berm, boasting zebra grass and sage, embraces
the steel machines that percuss beyond my bolted door.
Pity the expense of it all, the cost of repair, these rooms
requiring constant care. I am, at last, the empty bottle,
green glass streaked by runnels that mark the end
of a vessel's use, cork cracked. I arm myself
with the hammer and claw, nail loose fence boards
in plumbed relief, paint eight years of stain away.
A cry is muffled in a sunrise kitchen. The air fogs,
clotted with fumes, words unspoken. A grackle swings
its light—touched wings beyond the panes that belong to me
only a little longer. The bird's ebony eyes shine as it beaks
upward into a finch—fled Texas sky. Words are useless,
so I rip the newspaper to bits. Its language dead, stripped
of meaning, pages catch the drips from the roller, the drops
from the brush. Tilting on a topography too weak to bear
my weight, I color the spaces neutral to please an
      unknown palate,
then press the sign that begs for release mid—point into the edged
and polished lawn. I wonder why the clay won't cleave
from south to north and take me, skidding, home.

JP Reese

Living in the Spin Cycle

It isn't actually a wrecked stock car. I just call it that, the top two floors occupied, and the lower 48 on fire. The mirror on the wall has mastered the technique of waiting graciously for someone to appear. Meanwhile, I listen to the insect—like buzz of my own blood in embarrassed silence. The only instruction is FOLLOW ALL INSTRUCTIONS. There are naked women everywhere. I don't think I'll be doing laundry.

Howie Good

drink
seasons
convenience stores
marriage
chores
personal grooming
budgets
interior decoration
gender
public transport
church
raising children
politics
guilty pleasures
future

Natural Beauty

blow dried by the wind,
sunshine adds sheen to skin
and lightens hair.

my natural look
costs nothing,
and looks like it –

natural look from the shops
comes in jars and tubes
and costs much.

my smile though,
my smile is 100% real
and it's free –
now that's priceless!

Carolyn Cordon

Mars

1
A plane had just finished dusting the field, rows of what looked like obscurely defective hearts. There was a quiet sense of celebration about the evening. Forget your password? the computer prompted. No, but I have often changed my world view.

2
The god of carnage shrugs as if trying to loosen a painful knot in his shoulder. Red, he says, means danger. He never says what black means. His flabby arms are sheathed in sleeves of tattoos like a Pacific Islander. Shadows and ghosts haunt the surrounding woods. It's what I get for speaking ironically to people who don't understand irony.

3
I'll grow a bald man's gray ponytail, and the future will be cruel and often difficult, dotted with burning peasant huts and starvelings staring out from behind barbed wire, but there'll be nice grass in the cemetery, and birds that'll sing when I strum a ukulele and donkeys that'll be loaded with poems.

Howie Good

Suburban Mythology

A formal house of antique white,
you've learned to be a neutral wife.
You wear your make-up tastefully,
serve his hors d'oeuvres gracefully.

The Southern Comfort tossed away,
your Peachtree manners here to stay,
night dreams devoid of fine cocaine—
no hustling in Atlanta's rain.

You drive the car pool SUV,
feed the homeless faithfully;
teach your children Bible verse,
explain that they should *never* curse.

Bright purple boots and cowboy hat
lie boxed behind the ball and bat.
A gold Amex assures you that
your figure won't devolve to fat.

In these long, ivory hours you swear
by plain, cream-colored outerwear
your personal shopper says to be
the height of taste, but underneath

lie shining nights when you would dance
at honkytonks and grab the chance
to glide into the parking lot,
astride your latest Lancelot.

When death's hand waves, perhaps you'll see
you've written your own eulogy:
A consummate suburban wife
succumbs to self—inflicted life.

JP Reese

Perspective

You say nostril hairs.
I say nose lashes.

Ron Campbell

Appearance

Can you see the grey edge to her hair colour?
The brand—name clothes despite welfare payments?
The wine now flows from the tetrapack.
Which coat to wear to the chemist's?

As the Wall stood, she was at her best,
And not only the Stasi took notice of that,
American soldiers asked her over,
But she didn't follow.

She wants to move back to Thüringen.*
Maybe there she can start again.

Claudia Bierschenk
translated from the German by Desmond Shortt

---

* Thüringen: German state, formerly in East Germany

drink
seasons
convenience stores
marriage
chores
personal grooming
budgets
interior decoration
gender
public transport
church
raising children
politics
guilty pleasures
future

Lean Years

Every night around midnight street peddlers appear on the sidewalk. Pieces of the wood used to make Jesus's cross sell for about a dollar. The worst offenders are those who promise to teach what they know can't be taught. But don't think of me as missing or far from everywhere. I'm right here, where Lee Harvey Oswald shot Abraham Lincoln and ghosts of snow gust across the empty road, the hope of sleep abandoned but the locomotive in the dream still burning.

Howie Good

Divestiture

Today the list seems endless
of the trinkets I can give away.
A wedding ring, a house,
a grand piano, clothes in disarray.

Your culinary library can stay——
I'll choose a book or two.
The mitre saw? The Philip's head?
Take them. I'll even leave the screws.

You say perhaps I'll reconsider
——promise me you'll change your ways.
It's much too late to supplicate——
the Volvo goes; Suburban stays.

The vodka bottles tempt you, don't they?
Stashed behind your office drapes.
Afraid I'll pack them? Wrong, my friend,
I only want a clean escape.

I'll take the bonds, the 401's
to raise our sons——your gun remains.
Perhaps you'll have the decency
to use it and blow out your brains

No, don't accuse. I'll be in touch,
I can't say how and won't say when.
It's really just become too much.
Divest me, dear. Begin again.

JP Reese

The Agreement

Night owns the sky but rents the stars from Day.
Day leases shadows from Night but has a binding contract
      with the sun.

Every Night owes Day one morning.
Every Day pays Night back with an evening.

Day has a limited partnership with Night to illuminate
      the moon.
Night promises Day to keep its interference with the sun to a
      bare minimum.

At dusk Night forecloses on day.
At dawn Day renews its option.

Day retains all rights to its fame.
Night is allowed its mystery.

Ron Campbell

Don't count on it!

Money comes in, money goes out,
bills must be paid, of that there's no doubt
But budgeting, well it can drive one mad.
You'd love to splash out, make yourself glad,

numbers then though, wouldn't add up,
as much as you try, the answer is 'Nup!'
So only spend what you can afford to pay back
and perhaps one day, way down the track

you'll gather a stack, a pile, of dough
then you can think of the places you'll go!
London or Paris, Jamaica, Mumbai
Berlin or Boston, so many, oh my!

Or perhaps stay home, give your cash a count
if you've stuck at it, there'll be a goodly amount.
With the money can come some fancy stuff,
you can buy and buy, 'til you have enough.

But watch for those, who'd help you spend,
many of them may be foe, not friend –
fair weather types seduced by your money
they'll rip you off and you'll feel like a bunny ...

Carolyn Cordon

Budget

After a life spent looking after
her children, she died
leaving nothing
for her
self

Claudia Bierschenk
translated from the German by Desmond Shortt

drink
seasons
convenience stores
marriage
chores
personal grooming
budgets
interior decoration
gender
public transport
church
raising children
politics
guilty pleasures
future

The Wide Side of the Bed

Camped in the hinterlands of this hotel bed,

Bivouacked above the covers,

Staring out across the sheets.

The opposite of akimbo,

Curled fetal as a fist,

There's a thunderhead of pillows

Above the wide side of the bed.

My own Ice Station Zebra,

My personal South Pole,

My five hundred thread count percale ice floe.

Was it something that I didn't say

Or something that I said?

Now I'm hunched on the horizon

Of the wide side of the bed.

The air conditioner is blowing

Out of the North, by the vent.

The bedside lamp's a lighthouse

But all my ships have sank.

Was it something that I didn't mean

Or something that I meant?

Staring at the unthawed distance

Of the wide side of the bed.

Ron Campbell

ticked off

dust and hair – human and dog
and stuff that the mutts bring in.
plenty of books, and winning ribbons,
hmm more dust there, don't look too close …

this decoration thing, doesn't do it for me,
others feel differently, I know.
but if the sun's out there shining
and the family's all well, I reckon that's enough.

health and well-being – tick
meaning and purpose in life – tick
love and happiness – tick
decorating the house ticks me off!

Carolyn Cordon

Interior Decoration

I recommend a slinky modern draught.
Let it swirl around the door
and 'nose' into every corner
for a gentle dispersal of dust.

The sky: let it look in on the bed
and break up that old light
with an appealling pattern
a 'playful', 'handful' of shadows.

What waterglass by the bed: genius!
Wait until the sunlight catches it
and then disrupt that crystalised cacophony
with your 'own' hand!

The radio: see how its mindless chatter
gently 'lifts' the mood of resignation,
of anguish, of isolation,
offset by the charmingly silent telephone.

Claudia Bierschenk
translated from the German by Desmond Shortt

You Tell Yourself ...

House guests do not investigate bags and boxes
stashed in closets while one's host is away.
Your mother taught you this as well.
No need to meet past lovers, lost friends.

There are reasons ghosts lie stacked and folded
in dark hollows, stashed away from the glow of stars.
You tell yourself you do not want to learn their lessons,
so closets are out; backs of cupboards, unfair game.

Ignore the queasy allure that itches
to crawl inside and embrace another's darkness,
to unearth the exact paper scrap of the past
that may tell you what it was that sliced sadness
into your lover's hazel eyes. Private things

lie tucked beyond neutral territory, in those spaces
behind sofas, beyond shuttered doors, between pages
of dog-eared books. They are red oak leaves
pressed and forgotten, drops of blood dried to rust.
They wait, but not for you. Yes. *Keep out,* you tell yourself.

Old words, curling photos just beyond your sight, hang
like baited hooks. Compelling, perhaps even forgotten
by your host, they dangle through the hours of this quiet day
to lie beyond the rules you cannot seem to break.
So, you tell yourself ...

Polite guests stick to perusing Bishop and Eliot;
they appreciate Seurat's garden in its black edged frame.
Perhaps the grey carpet needs attention, or you can
simply sit while the old dog licks your toes, braid ribbons of light
as they leak, weak and lemony, through his patio door.

Go shopping, tend his plants, make the bed with satin sheets,
freeze meals he will eat when you're gone, once again.
Leave notes and hope they do not end as fodder for another's
wonder. Remind yourself of your own boxed scraps of pain,
dark days you have saved, hidden beyond the safety of the light
he offers you.

No need for his past. You've collected your own.

JP Reese

An Armed Man Lurks in Ambush

1
A bird whistles like a bullet from a high-powered rifle. I pick up a stone and put it in my pocket just in case.

2
Jews are each given a brush and a can of paint and told to number the trees. It isn't raining, but later it might.

3
The arrival of a man everybody calls Red can only mean one thing — a baby will celebrate its birth with tears and anguish.

4
I take a piss against the wall, a wrinkled old woman peeking over my shoulder. The words "mushroom" and "music" are contiguous in most English dictionaries.

5
"Do what you feel," we tell each other and misaddress packages intended for India to China. The ground shakes at shorter and shorter intervals.

6
And such wind! Like a sword waving in glittering circles above our heads!

7
The train could leave at any moment. She has one foot on the platform, one foot in the air. Then I remember that cavemen depicted running animals by giving them eight legs.

8
Weeds and stones grow to monstrous proportions. The birds fly away as if there were actually someplace else to go.

9
Soldiers wore black uniforms, police wore brown. To get red, you need dust and haze. Pollution makes the sky so beautiful.

10
There are many empty chairs. Soon there will be more.

Howie Good

drink
seasons
convenience stores
marriage
chores
personal grooming
budgets
interior decoration
gender
public transport
church
raising children
politics
guilty pleasures
future

No Best in Show

I'm so glad my baby turned out to be a boy
the bump I had was a girl, my mum said,
and I thought so too. When the time came though,
the baby wasn't a Madeleine but a Jake instead,
and I was glad.

Who was I to face the trial
of before−school plaiting, with ribbons and things?
I, the one who'd chosen the wrong breed of dog
to take to the top of the show dog world −
Schnauzers need scissor skills I barely understand.

Years later, I look back at the ribbons won,
the friends made, and the hours spent
brushing, combing, scissoring, cutting,
plucking and preening dog hair,
while barely facing up to my own locks.

I failed really, at grooming a Schnauzer,
and with my own grooming,
I'm only red ribbon standard − second place
at best, and I have serious doubts
about even ranking that high...

Carolyn Cordon

Punch Lines

I'd hoped to have landed now,
bruised, but intact, a cigarette
burning the clench from my chest,
but I'm spinning in treetops
through fist–broken air. He
shouldn't have cut me; he loves
me, he claims, as the crust
of his spittle dries tight on my face.
The screen door is locked; maybe
He'll wake up soon. I sway
on the porch swing and sing
in my blood to the moon.

JP Reese

Trouble

Her body language was written in cursive.
Her smile a meticulous grimace.
He was in trouble.

He weighed the distance between them.
Memorized the blur of her.
Snow fell in the spaces where they weren't.

His gaze swerved up her curves and parked on the bridge
      of her nose.
A smile idled behind a corner of her mouth.
He was in trouble.

The terrain of her was all valleys and sudden, perfect peaks.
Her glance a kind of surgery.
He was in trouble.

He read novels in her eyebrows.
She flipped through him like a magazine.
He was in trouble.

He sidled.
She sauntered.
Trouble.

She didn't walk
She let the tides roll across the muscles of her hips and
      allowed them to move her.
He was.
In trouble.

They were so close he could smell his heartbeat on her.
(trouble, trouble, trouble)

They unmade love.
Made fuck their mutual verb.
He was in.

Trouble.

He took a breather.
She took a break.
She rolled on top of him
He was in trouble.

Then a single tear sneaked out of her face
       and landed directly on his eye.
She was in trouble too.

Ron Campbell

Only the Birds Know
What the Birds are Saying

The path was slow and dusty, barely a path at all, and when I got to the end, I still hadn't found a Mister Cash machine. It was a sunlit picture of hell, an arbitrary moral system, with illegal blue running lights and passages of plagiarized music, but no female gravediggers yet or specified stages of mourning. Oh, how I longed to tell somebody about the new sex position that the men's magazine called "Lying in a Dentist Chair." Everything must do after its own kind.

Howie Good

Break

The bags still heavy
with stones and shells
that looked so nice when wet.

Sunshine smiles fixed
in the camera,
proof of how good it was.

Silence cowers between them.

Claudia Bierschenk
translated from the German by Desmond Shortt

drink
seasons
convenience stores
marriage
chores
personal grooming
budgets
interior decoration
gender
public transport
church
raising children
politics
guilty pleasures
future

Foreign Parts

1

Slouched in my seat beside the window, I waited for the irritable rumbling of the train to resume. The conductor paced the platform, taking hurried little puffs on a cigarette. Rumors circulated among the passengers about cockneys vs. zombies. A mouth rimmed in salt pressed against my ear.

2

I came to a fence and climbed over it and then realized I had forgotten my bag on the other side. A bird fluttered up. I thought I was dead. I wished I was dying.

3

There were five men in the café with hats before them on the table. They murmured to each other while glancing frequently in my direction. Under one of the hats was a revolver. The sky tilted, but only for an instant.

Howie Good

Under–ground

The homeless man says sorry,
looks down as he recites his life
in the subway's thick heat,

commuters sheltered by newspapers
feign sleep.

No one looks –
he shuffles along
wishes everyone a blessed day.

Claudia Bierschenk

The Feast

We roll south from the Bridgeport line, past the blue noses in Fairfield and Westport, the mistake that is Stamford. Peeping into Greenwich, Manhattan's ermine-lined bedroom, we ride the express train into Grand Central for the Feast of San Gennaro.

Shawl-clad grandmothers waddle down Spring Street's
        cobbles, cloaked as black
as Catholic guilt, tiny feet stuffed like cannolis into Payless shoes. They pray their penance, heads bowed, carved rosaries
        swaying between arthritic fingers.

These blackbirds of faith congregate al fresco after evening mass at St. Patrick's. They perch on nineteenth-century stoops to sip espresso and dip almond biscotti, old ladies chattering about their God. Of course He is Italian.

Green, red and white banners blaze above narrow streets to announce September's arrival. Bright posters wave Ciao Baby! Mangia! We plunge into Manhattan's Indian summer, cash in hand. Deep-fried calamari, sausage and pepper sandwiches scent welcome on the humid breeze.

Booths erected mask sooty tenements and display portable grills and deep-fryers, warming to the dance of tourists who gobble frittate, calzones, spumoni and zabaglione. We come to hear music, breathe the garlic of Little Italy, drink mellow Chianti.

We win useless stuffed animals, give them away, dunk sad
clowns for a dollar. We eat hot zeppoles dipped in powdered
sugar from brown paper bags. There are t-shirts to purchase,
pick-pockets to avoid.

We stroll up Mulberry to Hester, filled with stromboli, nostalgia,
paper-cup wine. This annual shoulder-to-shoulder pilgrimage
of gimme caps and logo shirts offers temporary succor in a world
that slowly succumbs to conformity's siren song.

The corner table where Crazy Joe ate his last supper
        has vanished.
Umberto's metal kitchen door, where years of gawkers
        poked fingers
into bullet wounds was hauled to the dump long ago.

Seeking a cab, we walk by McDonald's, packed with eaters.
Children in stocking feet play reassuring games. The smell of
sizzling fries overpowers the exotic weave of flavors on the
Sicilian air. The young grow distant, move away. Fires of
tradition flicker, grow cold.

Our late night taxi hums into the station. The train for
        home awaits.
Perhaps next year will bring the Feast of "Mac the Big."
San Gennaro, roll over.

JP Reese

Swerve

Say you're standing at a bus stop.
Say there's a slight drizzle.
Say the street is making noises like snakes.

Say a tendril of your hair is sticking to your cheek like a
        thin black river.
Say the storm drain at your feet is clogged with Autumn.
Say the city is nothing but a nest of strangers.

Say there's a note in your pocket written in cyrillic.
Say your heart is semi strangled in your throat.
Say the curb is like an edge of an abyss.

Say something's nestled in your brain among the twisted alleys.
Say it slides along the pathways to your ears.
Say it licks the underside of your resolve.

Say a tiny tail pokes out from under every overcoat that passes.
Say you never hear the hiss of air brakes or the scream
        of a stranger.
Say you step up on the bus bound for somewhere else.

Ron Campbell

Heard and seen on the bus

It was many years ago,
but I'll never forget the image –
two rough-looking blokes
inhabiting the entire rear end,
of my bus home from work.

Rough toughness personified, until
I heard his voice, the shorter of them.
Without looking, I saw the tears
choking his voice – 'You never
told me it'd fuckin' hurt!'

I had to look then, what was it
could bring tears from one like him?
He was looking at something underneath
the bandage across his manly chest,
something with unnatural colours,

beautiful colours. I looked away again,
his tears, acid dripped on my heart,
his trembling lip and pained eyes
as he looked at the inked-on damage,
hurt me too, with betrayal's pain.

Carolyn Cordon

drink
seasons
convenience stores
marriage
chores
personal grooming
budgets
interior decoration
gender
public transport
church
raising children
politics
guilty pleasures
future

La Luz de la Salida

Spring roses bloom beyond the bedroom window; their canes stretch each petaled head toward a waking April sun. Inside, the room lies shadowed, thick with sudden silence.

Sitting on her bed, the old woman bends forward, stretches across the expanse to stroke her husband's cheek. Her fingertips touch his motionless arm, its paper-thin skin still precious, still warm.

Light from the hallway sheens an oil cross painted on the old man's forehead. The weary priest kisses his beads, rises from his knees, and walks toward the open window to watch for morning.

A spark darts and weaves through the death-disturbed air; it hovers above the priest's sleep-tousled hair. It flames and it flickers, then shoots past the roses in spangles of fire toward the day, just ahead.

JP Reese

Black Milk

1
I wore my funeral suit. The only thing I taught him, the old man said, was how to drink a fifth a day. A schoolgirl laughed behind her hand as my shoes filled up with milk and blood.

2
The great windows of the cathedral were missing their stained glass. Babushkas ran about, pulling fire alarms. This wasn't something I'd experienced before.

3
There was a mountain of twisted corpses, their eyes wide open, their throats outstretched in accusation. The firing squad stood off to one side. A dog dozed amid indecorous hints of daybreak.

Howie Good

Old Women Blues

Pale folded crinkles,
crystal-ringed fingers
on a tea cup.

Dry biscuits
in dry mouths.

The loose girdle of chairs,
a candle and a teddy bear.

The old familiar tune
buzzes in the room.

Did you ever dance with Jimmy?
That Jimmy,
He sure loved to dance.

Claudia Bierschenk
translated from the German by Desmond Shortt

Where do I go to worship?

An elaborate edifice, made by man
is not the place I visit when I feel
I must rise up and give thanks.
My religion is my own, with no book,
no rules made by men to divide
their property. Church is where people
are married, shown newborn to the world
in celebration, and shown the door
when their end comes. Church is filled
with people who mouth false piety
and sing praises to their invisible
and wrathful God who watches over them
in judgement. My god is Nature,
my place of worship is wherever man
has left a space for nature to show
her lovely face. My god rewards me
with warming sun, cleansing rain
and the glorious miracle of rainbows…

Carolyn Cordon

Why

Who is the artist
That made the perfect brush strokes
That are your eyebrows?

Who do I compliment
For the exquisite sauntriness
Of your gait?

Where do I go
To offer an offering
For the blessing of your pulse?

Who sprinkled those freckles on your cheeks?

What is the longitude and the latitude
Of the place I should show gratitude
For each of your earlobes?

Where do I kneel
To pay homage
To the perfect knobbiness
Of your knees?

Where exactly is the temple
Dedicated to your temples?

Who is the sculptor
Of the slope of your shoulders,
The decider of the circumference
Of your wrists?

Who dreamed you up?

And why did he inflict you
On me?

Ron Campbell

drink
seasons
convenience stores
marriage
chores
personal grooming
budgets
interior decoration
gender
public transport
church
raising children
politics
guilty pleasures
future

How to get your teenager to listen

Once their children attain a certain age
parents despair of getting their message through.
It seems the teen hears nothing at any stage
and obeys not one of their often stated rules.

You may not realise the dangers of your task,
if obedience is what you want, listen well –
you may receive more than what you ask,
they may obey once and then take flight.

Your teenaged son or daughter is like you were,
do you remember living way back then?
A hormone-ridden troubled swearing cur,
taking offence at every single word.

All you were told was laden with hidden meaning,
so you strove to find just what it was they wanted.
It seemed the adults were always lying and scheming
to ensure your thoughts and wants were never heard.

Heed that lesson, and maybe you'll get through,
one day you and child may connect again.
Ignore the lesson and then you're in the stew –
your existence then thrown totally out of order.

Try hard to cast back your mind to the time when
you were at your teenaged hormonal height –
things were shinier and more special then,
richly golden and brighter than any star.

Or the entire world was cloaked with dankest mist
with you in the centre but trapped and unable to reach
the special one you'd only ever kissed.
He kissed and told tales, confidences breached.

Then the whole world knew, or thought they did
what both of you tenderly saw and felt and touched,
so you crawled to a hole, covered yourself and hid
not knowing why you loved that creep so much.

Remember that, and how it made you groan,
and you'll know what your child is going through right now
and why these things are for them to do alone –
they'll face trouble and win, and then come back to you.

You'll talk and realise times don't really change
as your child explores the choices that they have.
Listen to your child, and re–arrange
the things you both mistakenly thought you knew.

Carolyn Cordon

Heart Dent

Old soul died young.
Set in your ways by the age of four.
Crotchety at seven.
Downright Cantankerous at ten.
And then you died at eleven.
And maybe that was why
You seemed like such an old soul.

Wide eyes born open.
My eyes, staring back at me
And beyond and around me
Agog and agape.
Gobbling up the big everything.
Surprised at the world.
Brows arched, wide eyes.

Each breath counting as one less.
When the day came.
And the last one was spent.
And I died a little too
While the ghost of you flitted
In my peripheral vision.
Cursed to outlive you with each breath.

Heart dented, un mended.
You left without a note.
No warning, no prep.
Only the waves to counsel me
Along a shore you would have to leave un run.
But I keep your leash and collar
Trudge solo, heart dented.

Ron Campbell

Reconstruction

I told you; I sneaked inside the morgue
and touched the cloth that lined Grandfather's coffin.
It was cool and soft, like pebbles.
His folded hands were frosted, and
something had put a smile on his face.

Claudia Bierschenk

Side Effects

The children were there,
then they weren't.
Only a faint scar remained.
The hotline that was
supposed to help exploded.

And these weren't
the most serious side effects.

The air was full of people.
I sat alongside a weeping woman,
patting her hand,
the bread of affliction.

Howie Good

8 am

This is the story of how you lean in the doorway,
cheek bones etched with turquoise crayon.
Lines snake across your forehead; crude arrows
slide over the knobs of your shoulders.

You have prepared for war while I slept
through the small hours of this summer night.
You've protected your brain with a striped hat,

fur-lined earflaps and brim. Pom-pom ties sway
across your hollow chest. I smell smoke
on your breath, stale Budweiser on your clothes.

Your sleeveless t-shirt is the same faded black
you wore yesterday. Clavicles rise in sharp angles
beneath night-white skin.

I know you've been gone again and are still traveling
away from me. Your lips peel and flake, arms hang
at your waist: thin, blue-veined, sad.

This is the story of how I want to brush the dust
from the clocks, lift the heavy curtains from your eyes.
I picture the piping voice and gleaming face

of a three year old boy gazing up at me
and grinning a freckled grin, showing me
his sandbox castle with its protective moat.

This is the story that says I want to close
the bedroom door, escape from your ashen
presence to what might have been. But instead,

I smile from the distance of my chair,
nod my head when you pause for a moment
between flights of ideas. I want to know

what to do, tell you what pill to take, what pill
not to take, what thought to think, what fears
to shed, what book to read, what life to live,

how to be happy,
but I don't know any of this.
This is the story of what I long to do

but do not do. I want to gentle your tired
face, safe against my body, stroke
your matted hair, feed your disappearing flesh

and promise you all will be well. I want to repair
the broken places say I'm sorry beg forgiveness
for whatever this is I do not understand. Instead,

years of ghost words clot the air between us,
edges sharp as razors slicing veins,
and we cannot stumble through them

without blood. So you turn away, and I watch
you retreat up the stairs, to your war paint,
your empty bottles, your anger,

and I say nothing, but as I hear your tread
fade up the stairway, I pray that when you do finally
find sleep, you'll wake again to give us both another chance

to unearth the courage to speak of love,
of loss. But today, this frail glimmer
beneath silence and sorrow must suffice.

JP Reese

drink
seasons
convenience stores
marriage
chores
personal grooming
budgets
interior decoration
gender
public transport
church
raising children
politics
guilty pleasures
future

The real thing

Arms folded, feet together,
backs straight,
our throats filled
with countless yawns.

The teacher recited the day's
Russian words:
druzhba, mir, pobyeda
friendship, peace, victory,
when a familiar wailing
burst our daydreams:

Each time, the siren broke
our apathy with a gasp
and held its tune for minutes
more urgent than the
short−breathed fire drill.

This was different,
because we could take our time
(three minutes) down to the basement

where the little ones
huddled in tears,
because they thought
this was it − this was the *real* thing;
they'd never see their mothers again.

It was pleasantly creepy
to watch older students
run around in gas masks,
fake hand grenades
dangling on their belts.

They didn't look scared,
they would be in charge
when it *really* happened.

They looked like they couldn't wait
to get their hands on the Americans!

And we couldn't wait to be like them
(or so we said).

Until then, we'd practice the real thing
again and again and again.

Claudia Bierschenk

Haiku About Politics

Started my campaign
Running for your orifice.
Only need one vote.

Ron Campbell

What can I do?

My mind is open, my politics Green,
becoming more strident as I have grown.
By the end of my time who can tell
what I'll become? I'll wait until
the world has moved to the place I seek,
where people don't follow around like sheep
to chase the latest thing in droves.
This is the thought that truly drives
me – the ovine hordes make me angry –
they're all stuffed full, while others die hungry.
But what can I do? My words don't rate –
all I can do is sit here and write.

Carolyn Cordon

2008, What I Wanted

I wanted it to be 2007, before my husband lost
his white collar and our nest egg broke its shell against
the blind windows of Wall Street. I wanted not to feel
the clench in my guts every time the bills came due.
I wanted to believe my son, almost grown, would head
to college and enjoy the life my parents provided me.
It is 2011. My son works overnights. Mornings at seven,
I hear him climb the stairs toward his day's rest.
If I am quick, I may catch a trace of his boy's smile,
testing itself against an older, stranger's face.

JP Reese

Ypres
for Sarah M. & Tom C.

Despite
a cold
misty rain

poplars
stand
at attention

as

we wander
jet—lagged

down rows
& rows
of gravestones

40,000

stubby
white teeth

bared

Howie Good

drink
seasons
convenience stores
marriage
chores
personal grooming
budgets
interior decoration
gender
public transport
church
raising children
politics
guilty pleasures
future

Albert, Thirty Years On

Some midnights, the world stills,
its spinning slips, its axis tilts
toward memory. Be careful
where you step--The road to midnight
is carved in widening cracks, splits
that trap you between now
and then.

One friend fell in at 3:00. His skin
intact, his hair a golden gleam.
I remember 6:00, but suddenly
it's 9:00 pm, and darkness
brushes ash across my face.

At 6:00 my life would never end,
it stretched beyond Miami's sky,
and Biscayne Bay was at my back
to cool me when my dancing
partners changed.

The record player spun its hits
'til Albert tossed cocaine
across the spinning disc. Our skins
stripped, electric in their longing.
At 12:00, he said "I'm starved,"

rose from the bed and found,
(how odd), instead of bread
or cabernet, he turned his face
away from me and ate
his waiting, one−eyed,
blue−black gun.

JP Reese

Nibbled and sipped

Chocolate and red wine
reach out to me,
tickle my mind's palate
and lead me on.
On to a place of wonder,
where tongue and tummy
glory in taste and texture,
pleasure long denied,
now embraced.

So what if it leads
to an increased girth?
Pleasure, surely, is a worthy goal?
Guilt will ensure pleasure
is tightly reined in,
tasted now and then,
nibbled and sipped, lady—like,
not guzzled and gulped,
like a boar …

Carolyn Cordon

The Phantom Museum

1
Despite the time of day, night seems to be falling. America's most famous serial killers howl like Siberian wolves. There's nobody there who knows CPR, & it's too hot to go for help. The heat has the small, hooded eyes of Joan of Arc's inquisitor. She's sitting by herself at a table in the corner, hands covering her face.

2
The gendarmes approach with dicks hanging out. A century before, Van Gogh was locked up in the madhouse for touching the local women. The street where it happened has been restored. Tell everybody – all business is piracy.

3
On a Friday in August, Christopher Columbus sailed west into the unknown. His country was the future. Now we know that no revolution can achieve what evolution can't. Just give me a flashlight & a drawstring bag, & leave a car in the parking lot unlocked, & when I'm done rummaging, let me slip away like water, a silver bracelet with blue stones.

Howie Good

Eraser

I mourn the loss of erasers.
Now we just hit the delete button.
But with an eraser there was a rhythm,
A cadence to the task.

You make a mistake.
There is the brief exhale
Like a quick sigh
To expel the tiny frustration.

Then there's the eraser itself.
The feel of it.
Erasers are the cousins of rubber bands.
Everyone knows this.

Then there's the rubbing.
And The Disappearing Act.

And then the small finger of the left hand flicks once,
Then twice,
The tiny rolls of spent eraser.

And then the soft blow
To disperse them.
And then it all starts again until the next mistake.

And again,
Exhale.
Rub.
Flick.
Flick.
Blow.

And then the writing, writing, writing—
Mistake.
Exhale.
Rub.
Flick.
Flick.
Blow.

My delete button thinks I'm crazy.
He says writing is not dancing.
Anymore.

Ron Campbell

Justice

At the flea market
I buy a book for 50 cents.

In the café
I celebrate with coffee and cake.

A man comes in begging for change.

I turn my back on him
and write a poem.

Claudia Bierschenk
translated from the German by Desmond Shortt

drink
seasons
convenience stores
marriage
chores
personal grooming
budgets
interior decoration
gender
public transport
church
raising children
politics
guilty pleasures
future

Changes for a better poetic future

If I had blonde hair, I think
my career would be
quite different.

I'm not a tall person you see,
I'm very much
not tall.

But if my hair was blonde, I suspect
I'd gain a centimetre
or two

in height and people would
notice me much more
than they do

as I am right now, reddish brown
hair, and not at all
terribly tall.

My blonde hair would catch
the photographer's lens
and there I'd be

a slightly taller blonde person
looking blondly sophisticated
and oh so cool.

I'm convinced my poetry submission
strike rate would improve
almost immediately ...

Or barring a change in hair colour
perhaps I could have
a sex change

and a name change as well.
I'd join the mighty crew
and call myself

Jeff with a J or alternately
Geoff with a G. I reckon
that'd work

even better than changing my hair
from reddish brown
to blonde.

Carolyn Cordon

For Rebecca

This is the dark hour of your mother's song.
The scattered ashes fall. How to continue?
Your music drifts, you're in her mind, but gone.

You leave your scent on sheets, pictures you've drawn.
The sky denied, today dawns black, not blue.
This is the dark hour of your mother's song.

Your loved ones try to mask their devastation.
The children left behind, the older two
hear music call, you're in their minds, but gone.

A picture from September brings her longing,
a ribboned dress, your violin, your shoe.
This is the dark hour of your mother's song.

Dark clouds scud low to brush the shadowed lawn.
Each morning hones a sharper blade of truth.
Dawn's music troubles and reminds you've gone.

Rebecca, glitter, flutter off alone.
The earth offers a space for only you.
This is the dark hour of your mother' song.
The music drifts. You're in her mind. You've gone.

JP Reese

The Fisherman

On Awaji Island I watched as a fisherman mended his net. For several minutes I stood there as he worked. Watched silently as his blunt and nimble fingers did their ancient choreography, filling the gap one tiny square at a time where some of his catch had slipped like a shiver of silver to roam another day in the icy Inland Sea. He used his teeth to cinch the frayed ends and he had taken his shoe off and was using his big toe to pull the line taut. After a while he sensed me standing there and looked up. Our eyes met and his shifted a little but like Elizabeth Bishop's fish it was not to return my stare. He bent back to the task, hunched the way men have hunched for a thousand years. I stood there, admiring his sullen fingers, the crane of his neck, his uncomplicated immersion. And like a tourist from the future, I snapped a picture of him on my smartphone and walked away.

Ron Campbell

In the Dark

1
Ask anyone how they found themselves living in this country, & they'll tell you which common household objects can get you high. Hardly anyone mentions just how much suffering healing is.

2
The next day only brings more rain & incompetent boots. Not a single unborn child objects.

3
Charred corpses litter the streets. Imagine, if you can, blowing white curtains, a black hole with teeth.

Howie Good

Logic

The future was better in the past,
the past is better at present,
and the present will be so much better in the future.

Cynicism is all the hype.

Claudia Bierschenk

Poems, listed

drink

An American in Belgium	Howie Good	16
Club Mate	Claudia Bierschenk	18
Recipe	Ron Campbell	19
Achieving Sobriety	JP Reese	20
Our little secret	Carolyn Cordon	21

seasons

Crash	Ron Campbell	24
Affliction	Claudia Bierschenk	25
Autumn	JP Reese	26
Autumn Sonata	Howie Good	28
Why did the snake cross the road?	Carolyn Cordon	29

convenience stores

the inconvenience store	Carolyn Cordon	32
Catch Trap	JP Reese	33
To the Blue	Howie Good	34
Transit	Claudia Bierschenk	35
Inconvenience Store	Ron Campbell	36

marriage

Operators	Ron Campbell	38
night time struggle	Carolyn Cordon	40
Love Surrounds Us Like a Posse …	Howie Good	41
Ghosts	JP Reese	42
Marriage	Claudia Bierschenk	44

chores

Rush hour	Claudia Bierschenk	46
Not a Housewife	Carolyn Cordon	47
The Day I Don't Wake Up	Ron Campbell	48
Topos	JP Reese	50
Living in the Spin Cycle	Howie Good	51

personal grooming

Natural Beauty	Carolyn Cordon	54
Mars	Howie Good	55
Suburban Mythology	JP Reese	56
Perspective	Ron Campbell	58
Appearance	Claudia Bierschenk	59

budgets

Lean Years	Howie Good	62
Divestiture	JP Reese	63
The Agreement	Ron Campbell	64
Don't count on it!	Carolyn Cordon	65
Budget	Claudia Bierschenk	66

interior decoration

The West Side of the Bed	Ron Campbell	68
ticked off	Carolyn Cordon	70
Interior Decoration	Claudia Bierschenk	71
You Tell Yourself…	JP Reese	72
An Armed Man Lurks in Ambush	Howie Good	74

gender

No Best in Show	Carolyn Cordon	78
Punch Lines	JP Reese	79
Trouble	Ron Campbell	80
Only the Birds Know…	Howie Good	82
Break	Claudia Bierschenk	83

public transport

Foreign Parts	Howie Good	86
Under–ground	Claudia Bierschenk	87
The Feast	JP Reese	88
Swerve	Ron Campbell	90
Heard and seen on the bus	Carolyn Cordon	91

church

La Luz de la Salida	JP Reese	94
Black Milk	Howie Good	95
Old Women Blues	Claudia Bierschenk	96
Where do I go to worship?	Carolyn Cordon	97
Why	Ron Campbell	98

raising children

How to get your teenager to listen	Carolyn Cordon	102
Heart Dent	Ron Campbell	104
Reconstruction	Claudia Bierschenk	106
Side Effects	Howie Good	107
8 am	JP Reese	108

politics

The real thing	Claudia Bierschenk	112
Haiku About Politics	Ron Campbell	114
What can I do?	Carolyn Cordon	115
2008, What I Wanted	JP Reese	116
Ypres	Howie Good	117

guilty pleasures

Albert, Thirty Years On	JP Reese	120
Nibbled and sipped	Carolyn Cordon	122
The Phantom Museum	Howie Good	123
Eraser	Ron Campbell	124
Justice	Claudia Bierschenk	126

future

Changes for a better poetic future	Carolyn Cordon	128
For Rebecca	JP Reese	130
The Fisherman	Ron Campbell	131
In the Dark	Howie Good	132
Logic	Claudia Bierschenk	133

Poets

Claudia Bierschenk

Claudia Bierschenk's poetry has been published in *Juice Press*, *Full of Crow*, *Public Republic*, *Alittlepoetry*, *Durable Goods*, and *SAND Journal*. Her first poetry chapbook *Perestroika Silence* was published by erbacce Press, Liverpool in 2010, and her work has also featured in several poetry anthologies by ForwardPress, Peterborough (UK). Claudia has been previously nominated for the Pushcart Poetry Prize and for Best of the Net. She won 3rd place at the 2011 Berlin Poetry Awards. Claudia lives in Berlin.

Ron Campbell

Ron Campbell is a poet, playwright and actor, born in Santa Monica, California and based in San Francisco. He makes his living touring the world as a clown with Cirque du Soleil. Ron received the Fox Fellowship for Distinguished Achievement in 2010 and is the author of two collections of unwritten poetry, *The Detourist* and *In Corrigible,* and has had work published in *Flutter Poetry Journal*, *Psychic Meatloaf Contemporary Poetry Journal* and *Mipoesias Poetry Journal*. Ron is a performer of several one-man shows including *R. Buckminster Fuller*, *The History (and Mystery) of the Universe*, *The Thousandth Night*, *Shylock*, *Shipwrecked* and *The Boneman of Benares*. More of Ron's works may be seen at his website *Scrutinies & Tangentia*: http://roncampbell.posterous.com/

Carolyn Cordon

Carolyn Cordon is a poet and writer, wife and mother, and dog lover. She is also writing her first memoir, in verse, telling her story about how Multiple Sclerosis (MS) has changed things for her. Life is still moving forward, but more slowly now, and in a more deeply considered way. Writing, for Carolyn, has been therapy to keep some kind of mental control over her body, which is behaving badly! Writing about it all helps. Find her blog here: http://carolyn-poeticpause.blogspot.com.au/

Howie Good

Howie Good, a journalism professor at SUNY New Paltz, is the author of five poetry collections, most recently *Cryptic Endearments* from Knives Forks & Spoons Press. He has had numerous chapbooks published, including *Elephant Gun* from Dog on a Chain Press, *Strange Roads* from Puddles of Sky Press, and *Death of Me* from Pig Ear Press. His poetry has been nominated multiple times for the Pushcart Prize and Best of the Net anthology, and his blog can be found at http://apocalypsemambo.blogspot.com.

JP Reese

JP Reese has poetry, fiction, creative nonfiction, book reviews, and writer interviews published or forthcoming in many online and print journals such as *Metazen, Blue Fifth Review, A Baker's Dozen: Thirteen Extraordinary Things,* and *The Pinch*. Reese is an Associate Poetry Editor for *Connotation Press: An Online Artifact* (http://connotationpress.com/) and an editor for *Scissors and Spackle* (http://www.scissorsandspackle.com/). Cervena Barva Press has scheduled Reese's second poetry chapbook, *Dead Letters*, for publication in 2013. Her published work can be read at *Entropy: A Measure of Uncertainty* (http://jpreesetoo.wordpress.com/).

145

Acknowledgments

Claudia Bierschenk

Thank you, Desmond Shortt, not just for translating.
And thank you, Matt Potter, for being interested, supportive, and honest.

Ron Campbell

My thanks to editors Matt Potter, George McKim, Sandy Benitez and Dulce Menendez.
"Recipe" appeared on *Mipoesias* online journal.
"Heart Dent" is dedicated to Carny.

Carolyn Cordon

I offer a huge thank you to Matt Potter, the wonderful editor who rounded up the poets for this fascinating project, and who kept us all headed in the correct direction. A posse of poets isn't the easiest of things to control, but Matt has done it, and done it well!
"Natural Beauty" and "Why did the snake cross the road?" were performed at the Gawler Poets at the Pub poetry readings in 2012.
"Why did the snake cross the road?" was also read on Triple B FM – Barossa Community Radio

Howie Good

I would like to thank the editors of *Bareback Lit*, *Saudade*, *New Verse News*, *New Towner* and *Rufous City*, where some of these poems previously appeared in an earlier form.

JP Reese

"La Luz de La Salida" and "Autumn" will appear in *Dead Letters*, a poetry chapbook, forthcoming in 2013 from Cervena Barva Press.

"2008, What I Wanted" was published by *Wilderness House Literary Review* and *Poets on the Great Recession* in 2012.

www.ingramcontent.com/pod-product-compliance
Lightning Source LLC
LaVergne TN
LVHW011355080426
835511LV00005B/296